I can see

a cat

walking on the fence.

I can see

the washing

blowing on the line.

I can see

a man

cutting the grass.

I can see
a dog
burying his bone.

I can see
a butterfly
sitting on a flower.

I can see

a spider

making his web.

I can see
the birds
feeding at the table.

I can see
all these things
from the kitchen
window.